What to Write in a Birthday Card

What to Write in a Birthday Card

Sayings for Cards or Text Messages

Self-Published

by Barbara Tremblay Cipak

Copyright

Self Published by Barbara Tremblay Cipak, Toronto, Ontario, Canada
Copyright © 2019.

All rights reserved.

No part of this book may be used or reproduced for commercial use in any manner whatsoever without written permission except in the case of brief quotations embodied in articles or reviews.

These Sayings can be used in personal cards for personal use or sent as a personal text message.

Barbara (Tremblay) Cipak has written all the sayings for cards in this book. Any sayings that resemble people, characters, businesses, organizations, places, events, other sayings, are coincidental.

For information contact: admin@drageda.com, Barbara Cipak, Toronto, Ontario Canada

ISBN: 9781707965045
What to Write in a Birthday Card – Sayings for Cards or Text Messages

Disclaimer: Terms of Use:

These suggested sayings for cards or text messages are not meant to encourage or to be used for harassment or passive-aggressive hate, or direct-hate towards people who do not wish to receive cards or texts. These sayings are written for, and intended for mutual, consenting relationships. By using these sayings, in part or whole, for cards or texts, you are acknowledging and agreeing to these terms of use.

Dedicated

To

Everyone who has a birthday, wait, that's the entire human race. If today is your big day, Happy Birthday!

Acknowledgements

"For this book, I'd like to acknowledge my hubby, who managed to find me the best desk! Without this desk, this book and the recent other three, may not have happened. Powerful desk."

How to Use These Sayings

There are multiple uses for '*What to Write in a Birthday Card.*'

Go ahead and use these sayings as-is for personal use. Of course, you can modify them for your personal use as well.

To Help You Write Something in a Blank Card

If you're like most people, stuffed in a drawer somewhere are numerous unused blank cards. Use these sayings to inspire you to write something inside those cards.

Perhaps you've decided to make a custom card for someone special, but need a bit of inspiration to determine what to write inside. Again, use this book to tap into your creative side.

Send Them Out as a Text Message to Someone You Love

If you can't think of what to text to the birthday person, refer to the book. Pick out a saying that says what you want, or modify it to suit your personal needs.

Table of Contents

Dedicated..4

Acknowledgements..5

How to Use These Sayings..6

Funny Sayings for a Card..8

Thoughtful Sayings for a Card..24

Inspirational Sayings for a Card...39

Sarcastic Sayings for a Card...57

Cheerful Sayings for a Card..78

About The Author...96

Why A Book About Sayings for Cards?..................................97

Thank You for Reading...98

Funny Sayings for a Card

Chapter One

(1)
"Happy navel separation day!"

(2)
"You're not old, you're incredibly experienced."

(3)
"At the time of your birth, the heavens parted, then the clouds formed, and strangely enough, after that, there was a burst of laughter."

(4)
"Today, you get forgiven for wearing socks and sandals. You get one day only!"

(5)
"For your birthday, all you're getting is this card, an unlimited credit card. Do I really need to put the lol in there?"

(6)
"You're not growing older, you're growing wiser. Just wondering if you're wise to the fact that you're getting old?"

(7)
"For your birthday, I want you to come over and cook me dinner, that way I can give you compliments while you cook. That's your gift. You're welcome."

(8)
"I have the perfect gift for you. When you see me next I'm giving it to you personally. You might not see me for maybe ten years. It's going to spoil, I better eat it now. I'll think of you though."

(9)
"Don't think your birthday is special, just because you're an amazing, attractive, smart, one-of-a-kind soul who happens to be the most generous person I know. Did I mention you're the idol of my eye, and everything you do is perfect? I need to borrow money, how am I doing?"

(10)
"We're having a surprise party for your birthday, SURPRISE! You're not invited. We know how you hate those things."

(11)
"Come over, and I'll whisper sweet nothings in your ear. Literally."

(12)
"You're not growing older, you're shrinking older, get it right!"

(13)
"When I dream, I dream of the fact that you're still frigging older than I am, yippee!"

(14)
"I put a big bow on myself today for your birthday, darn near choked myself, hope you appreciate the effort."

(15)
"My horse counted your age today with his leg, he's now officially arthritic."

(16)
"In your hour of need, I'm here for you, happy omg-I'm-so-old-day"

(17)
"Be a happy fool on your big day. Walk around with a crazy smile just to freak everyone out."

(18)
"I'm going to make *time* for you on your birthday. In a bowl, I'll be mixing youth serum, a good attitude, and two teaspoons of brain brightening sugar. Eat this, and in the morning, you'll wake up at the age of five again. The downside, check the bed, you might have peed. Oh wait, you do that now, so no biggie."

(19)
"You can do anything, why is that! You can even age without aging! Would you cut the rest of us some slack and stop being wonder woman. We can't compete with you and all your talents. Happy birthday to the one we love to hate."

(20)
"Most of the time you're loopy, but on your birthday you get away with it so be loopier today."

(21)
"You get older and look hotter, we get older and look like crap, you piss us all off."

(22)
"Wrinkles remind us we're still here, like that's the kind of reminder we want, so happy wrinkle reminder day."

(23)
"May all your wishes come true, even that nasty one you're wishing for right now."

(24)
"Don't be the kind of person who never ages; we all hate those people."

(25)
"You're young and fiercely good looking, we remember how that feels, enjoy it while it lasts!"

(26)
"If you want to be the person you can be, stop looking younger every year, you're torturing all of us."

(27)
"When you get to be 100, beam us up to your space car, and we'll party at warp speed."

(28)
"We're not wasting any of our time celebrating your birthday, you're too damn perfect and we're jealous as all hell, hope you're happy!"

(29)
"Set your soul free on your big day but don't get arrested, we can't afford the bail."

(30)
"You're like coffee; hot, bold and you perk us up."

(31)
"We all love you, but face it, we're all scared of you!"

(32)
"The entire planet should celebrate your birthday because that about sums up the size of your ego! But that's why we love you."

(33)
"Don't cry because you're a year older, it could be worse, I could be a year older."

(34)
"A glass of wine, actually hard liquor, can cure the birthday blues. It's not right to drink alone, so you may as well share it with the rest of us. We promise to be happy drunks and help you out of your funk."

(35)
"Lookup in the sky, pick a star, make a wish, then laugh, because only dingbats believe in that crap, happy birthday dingbat."

(36)
"You're too nice to be another year older, only nasty people age!"

(37)
"We're all walking the plank of life, on the upside you're still walking, happy birthday."

(38)
"Celebrate your day, by being the best version of yourself, actually that's more of a gift for us!"

(39)
"You are trouble, and we're a bit twisted because we love trouble."

(40)
"Today is your happy day, so please do us a favor and follow the rules and actually be happy."

(41)
"Can you remember that most of us aren't as amazing as you, happy birthday to the one who stole all the talent."

(42)
"Just stop having birthdays, we're tired of telling you you're awesome."

(43)
"You're shallow, annoying, difficult, and for whatever reason, it suits you! Happy birthday, we're glad you're you."

(44)
"Do whatever you want today, except for that! Don't do that! Nevermind, go ahead and do it, but film it. We'll make a fortune if it goes viral. Happy Birthday, Hell-Raiser."

(45)
"Stop and smell the roses; they'll be shocked to see you. The last time they had a good look at you was on your wedding day nearly 100 years ago!"

(46)
"It's your birthday, so it's time to let loose and be the person you've always wanted to be. I'll run your bath and put out your pajamas for 9 pm. You're not exactly the wild-one!"

(47)
"I'm taking you out on the town tonight; let's get arrested. On second thought, you get arrested, I'll pay the bail. Happy birthday, that's my gift."

(48)
"Hotties who have birthdays have to buy us normal people a gift; we're happy you're older but pissed that you still look so good."

(49)
"You know all my secrets, that's why I have to send you a birthday card every year; can't risk you turning on me!"

(50)
"Instead of *the* present, I got you *the* future, your own plot of land on Mars. Just a tiny hiccup, we can't get you there. Put it in the Will, in 200 years someone in your family will really like me."

(51)
"You are the reason I drink, so let's drink together on your annoying birthday! Just kidding, you know I love you most of the time, right?"

Thoughtful Sayings for a Card

Chapter Two

(52)
"Your birthday is a time for us to stop and take a minute to thank you for being you, we love you"

(53)
"You do so much for so many and sometimes we, the many, forget to properly thank you. Making your birthday happy is the least we can do!"

(54)
"This crazy world is a little less crazy because you're in it, happy birthday."

(55)
"You shine brightly in our hearts, in fact, your aura is so bright we should all wear sunglasses around you."

(56)
"You're my peace of mind, thank you for being in my life, happy birthday."

(57)
"You have mastered living life with kindness and heart; we are so lucky to have you in our lives, happy birthday."

(58)
"I can't believe you're in my life; you are one of the most decent people I have ever known, happy birthday."

(59)
"Summer days remind me of you, calm, warm, inviting and beautiful, happy birthday."

(60)
"If there was ever a time to tell you you're special, your birthday is that time. Happy birthday to one of the most amazing people I know."

(61)
"I've traveled through time with you, and in this life, you're just as special as you were in all the others. I know, sounds crazy, right? But think about it, how could you be this spectacular without getting multiple lifetimes to practice in?"

(62)
"Dreaming brings me closer to you, wish we shared continents, happy birthday."

(63)
"If you were never born, a lot of people would be missing beauty in their lives, happy birthday."

(64)
"Your birthday is a time we all ask ourselves what did we do to deserve such a kind soul in our life."

(65)
"You need to volunteer for the first cloning experiments because the world would be more beautiful with multiple versions of you."

(66)
"Happy birthday to the brightest star on planet earth."

(67)

"Your heart is what we love about you; your kindness is what we love about you; your smarts are what we love about you. Let's face it; we love everything about you, Happy Birthday to the one who possesses all of life's positive traits."

(68)

"Nobody does it better, it's a cliche, but nonetheless, true. You're the best, happy birthday."

(69)

"Let's spend more time together this year. Sending birthday cards isn't nearly enough. Your birthday is the beginning of a new 1950s approach to living."

(70)
"Can you tell how much I love you? I don't think you can because I don't show you enough. Well let me take this time to tell you how incredible you are and how proud you should be for being who you are. I love you, happy birthday."

(71)
"For your birthday, I'm sending you hope, love, abundance, peace, faith, joy, and friendship. If you can think of the cliche, I'm sending it. As corny as that may be, it's what I want you to have. You deserve good things, and I want to make sure you understand how special you are. Have a great day."

(72)
"When your birthday comes around each year, I think about you and all you've done for me. It's my time marker and a reminder to tell you how much you're appreciated and loved, happy birthday."

(73)
"Some people are average, then there's you, riding above everyone high up in the clouds. We'll never catch up to your awesomeness, but that's ok, we realize your one-of-a-kind nature can never be duplicated, happy birthday."

(74)
"Happy Birthday to a beautiful soul, we love you."

(75)
"Happy birthday to the person who deserves a lot more than just people saying 'happy birthday.' You're always giving, wish I could give you the moon."

(76)
"You are connected to me, I'm connected to you, and for that, I'm grateful beyond words. Happy birthday to the person who helps me to breathe in and out every day."

(77)
"My favorite thing about life is you. There's nothing like having someone like you to turn to. I hope you know that you can turn to me as well."

(78)
"Wonder woman or Superwoman, neither hold a candle to all you do. Thank you for keeping everyone's life in order. You do so much, and we're baffled by your talents! Happy Birthday."

(79)
"Long-lasting love is the result of dedication, connection, and promises. You've mastered all of these, and for that reason, and many more, I love you, happy birthday."

(80)
"You're so intuitive; you can hear the drumbeat of my heart. How did I get so lucky, I love you, happy birthday."

(81)
"If you knew the way your support fed my soul, you'd have to charge me money. Your support has meant the world to me. Happy birthday to someone who deserves so much more on their special day."

(82)
"In my life, there has been one constant, and that constant has been you. Through all our trials, we stayed together, and you showed me what devotion truly means. Thank you for who you are and all you've done. I love you, happy birthday."

(83)
"I wake up each day thinking about how I can make your day better. What small thing can I do to show you how much you mean to me? I want you to be happy, and I want you to feel just how important you are. I love you, happy birthday."

(84)
"Life isn't just lists and tasks; life is people, connection, love, and friendship. You understand that better than anyone I know, and on your birthday, I want to take a minute to thank you for being such a thoughtful soul."

(85)
"You treat others with love and respect and, without knowing it, you're teaching us how to behave. You're an amazing example. Happy birthday to the best life teacher there is."

(86)
"The thing is, none of us are perfect, we're all just doing our best. Except you, you're doing more than most of us, thank you. Happy birthday."

(87)
"You shine bright; we love to be in your light. Keep shining; the world needs people like you. Your spirit is nourishment. Happy birthday."

(88)
"You started in life as the underdog and proved everyone wrong; you are my inspiration, happy birthday."

(89)
"Sharing this life with you has kept me grounded and sane, thank you for being the hope in my life, happy birthday."

(90)
"Time with you has been the greatest gift; I wish I could give us both more of it. If I could spend every lifetime with you, I would. I love you, happy birthday."

(91)
"When you open this card, you'll see what you mean to us. I'm sorry it's just a card that says, 'you mean everything to us.' Wish we could give you the world. Happy birthday awesome."

(92)
"You've been working so hard to achieve your dreams; my birthday wish for you is that they all come true. You deserve it. You are the definition of perseverance. Keep climbing mountains, and don't forget to wave from the top. Happy birthday."

Inspirational Sayings for a Card

Chapter Three

(93)
"Life hands us lemons so we can put them in the blender and make healthy smoothies. Take control of your life this year and turn all your bitterness into something sweet. Happy birthday."

(94)
"As we grow older, we learn that not knowing all the answers is ok, here's to leaving some things to the universe to worry about, happy birthday."

(95)
"There's something beautiful about celebrating our 365 day trip around the sun, here's to your next 365, happy birthday."

(96)

"All the great minds who came before us understood that in the end, it's the love we hold that we take with us; hope your year is filled with mountains of love. Happy birthday."

(97)

"Sunshine is Gods' way of energizing our soul so we can travel our journey with extra power beneath our feet. May you have an abundance of sun in your life. Happy birthday."

(98)

"It's ok to have fun in life, especially today. Set your soul free and joyfully celebrate. Happy birthday."

(99)

"Life isn't as complicated as we make it. On our birthday, we celebrate our entrance, but it's also a marker that reminds us to go for our dreams. Happy dream reminder day."

(100)

"Your dreams feed your soul, don't ever stop dreaming. Birthdays mark time, they are not the finish line. Take what is rightfully yours, your destiny."

(101)

"Our age has nothing to do with our dreams. Belief is the engine. Keep believing. Don't give up."

(102)
"Every road you traveled brought you to where you are today. Celebrate that road, because there's hope in the good and the bad. Your spirit is stronger than you know. Have a great year ahead."

(103)
"It's what we contribute during our lifetime that matters, and you've earned a gold medal in that department. Happy birthday."

(104)
"Your life is a reflection of your trials and successes. Congratulations on all you've accomplished. Happy birthday."

(105)
"The light of angels shine on you; you're blessed with many gifts. All of us notice your kind soul. Thank you for being you. Happy birthday."

(106)
"Our struggles are the lessons that help us move forward and turn a page to something better. You've been through a lot and deserve smooth sailing in the next chapter of life. Happy birthday, and we hope for only good things for you."

(107)
"You are a beautiful example of what grace means, thank you. Happy birthday."

(108)

"Keep being who you are and doing what you're doing. You've mastered life. Here's to another year of plowing forward and building dreams. Happy birthday."

(109)

"Keep yesterday out of your tomorrow. You've learned from experience, now build from there. Have a great year ahead. Happy birthday."

(110)

"Never let your setbacks stop you from chasing your dreams. Hold onto your strong mind and dedicated heart. You've earned everything you've achieved. Happy Birthday."

(111)
"Life is about movement, don't sit and wait for things to happen, go out and make them happen. Keep moving, sit less, plan more, do more. We are here to support you, so don't hesitate to ask for help. If there's anything we can do, we will. These are our birthday wishes for you this coming year."

(112)
"Life is an adventure. We seem to forget that anything worth having is worth working towards. Continue on your adventure; you deserve a multitude of good things. Happy birthday."

(113)
"A confident nature is appealing, and you're very appealing. We love you. Happy birthday."

(114)
"Don't let your age stop you from starting something new, or setting a new goal. If anyone can accomplish dreams, it's you. Have a wonderful year. Happy birthday."

(115)
"When you push through and take a baby step forward every day, you will have gone a mile without knowing it. Keep plugging away; you'll get there. Happy birthday."

(116)
"Inner peace is something we choose to welcome no matter what's going on in our life. I'm praying for you to have a year filled with good energy vibes to make it easier to tap into that inside joy. Happy birthday."

(117)
"Your birthday is the day the world was introduced to you. We're grateful for your entrance, and more than that, we're grateful that you're a part of our lives. Happy birthday to a special person."

(118)
"You're the best person I know."

(119)
"Your star shines inside all of us. We're lucky to have you to turn to. Your shoulders catch us all, and sometimes we feel that's not fair to you. However, you never complain, and you listen and advise us in our daily life with grace and kindness. There isn't anyone better than you in our books. We love you. Happy birthday.

(120)
"The truth is you're an outstanding person inside and out. Your dependable nature is incredible. When you were born, you were blessed with all the best character traits."

(121)
"Our inspiration comes from you."

(122)
"Hope keeps our heart open to anything being possible. You've held onto hope your entire life. It has lead you to where you are today. Your tenacity and trust is a lesson for all of us. Happy birthday."

(123)
"Faith is the ultimate guide in life. Hold onto faith in your God, faith in yourself, and faith in others, and you'll begin to see with your heart. Happy birthday."

(124)
"When you've trusted those worthy of trust, and most importantly, trusted in yourself, you've opened the door to peace. Happy birthday."

(125)
"You can plan, you can think, you can write it down, but your dreams don't have a chance until you take action. Be brave and go for it. Happy birthday."

(126)
"Keep your eyes and ears open more often than your mouth, and you'll get to where you're going with more knowledge than most. Have a great year ahead, happy birthday."

(127)
"Work hard to work smart. Getting ahead is as much about thinking as it is about doing. Plan your path, then take action. Have a wonderful year. Happy birthday."

(128)

"Dream big but find happiness and peace in the smallest things. When your pleasures come from natural places, like nature, animals, friends, and family, life maintains balance. We hope you have a successful and peaceful year. Happy birthday."

(129)

"Your age doesn't accurately measure time; it's just a number. Your age is how you feel inside about life and yourself. You should be proud; you're pretty damn amazing. Happy Birthday."

(130)

"You've climbed mountains, congratulations and happy birthday."

(131)
"We've caught a rising star; you. Keep working hard, stay grounded, and remember where you came from. In the end, it's the love we take with us. Keep love at the top of your list. We love you. Have another great year, happy birthday."

(132)
"Another trip around the sun means you get another chance to go for it. Take that chance! Happy Birthday."

(133)
"Your destiny is in the stars. Read the stars, follow the signs. Happy Birthday."

(134)
"Your birthday is the universe reminding you to plan your life and chase your dreams. Time is marching on, and your hopes matter. Have a great year, happy birthday."

(135)
"Here's to a life filled with sunshine. Pure light and all that's bright, that is our wish for you. Happy birthday."

(136)
"Taking the road less traveled requires a level of bravery that many people don't have. We believe you're the exception and will accomplish more than most. Have the best year ahead."

(137)
"Keep people in your life who inspire you and are positive about your goals. Positive people help you become all you can be. Surround yourself with that energy. Happy birthday."

(138)
"Your birthday reminds us that time is marching on. You're getting older, and so are we. Let's spend more time together in the coming year."

(139)
"If I could make your life pain free, I would. I don't want to see you travel a challenging path. Sorry, but I want it all to be easy for you. I love you, happy birthday."

(140)
"You can't really put a value on love, so don't. Remember that the love you give is a seed that grows. Plant lots of seeds this coming year. Leading with love helps the world and brings you peace. Happy birthday."

(141)
"When you approach your day with a smile, you notice happy people. Your smile inspires smiles. We hope you receive and give a lot of smiles in the coming year. Happy birthday."

(142)
"Your life is a living example of beauty and grace. Happy birthday"

Sarcastic Sayings for a Card

Chapter Four

(143)
"You're old, so don't try anything that'll break a hip! Happy don't-break any-bones-day."

(144)
"You're still a young thing. Compared to us, you're a Zygote. Google it. Happy birthday!"

(145)
"Don't get cocky on your birthday, just because you're a stud, and we all want to be you! Nevermind, go ahead and rub our noses in your perfection! Happy birthday anyway."

(146)
"Stop aging, it sucks! Happy birthday anyway."

(147)
"Apparently, you're a diva, which means this card probably won't meet your standards. Sorry your Highness, signed one of your peasants. Happy diva day!"

(148)
"Didn't you just have a birthday? Is the earth spinning faster or something? Let's get the hell off of this merry-go-round!"

(149)
"You're a handful of trouble, and we're scared about what you have planned to celebrate your big day. So don't mind the bullet-proof vests we're wearing. Happy birthday, go easy on us!"

(150)
"It's your birthday, and we're already freaking exhausted! What do you have planned this year, do we need bodyguards again?"

(151)
"Don't do anything that will get you arrested this year, we're out of bail money. Happy birthday to prisoner number 232."

(152)
"Open your mind to the idea that you're no longer a spring chicken, you're just a chicken! Don't be scared, it's only a freaking birthday. If nothing calms you, drink wine."

(153)
"You know that old saying, 'still waters run deep?' you're more like a puddle. Happy birthday to the uncomplicated one!"

(154)
"We measure your success by your talent, because your bank account is on life support! Here's to a full recovery this year, happy birthday."

(155)
"Your birthday is a giant plot to get gifts, adoration, money, and congratulations; we're not falling for it this year. All you're getting is this card, filled with words, like happy birthday gorgeous, here's a bunch of cash. Damn. Got us again."

(156)
"Let's travel through time for your birthday. We'll try not to erase ourselves."

(157)
"Your birthday is the excuse we use to party too hard. Just wondering why you have one every week?"

(158)
"Have you ever been so frustrated with someone you could scream? Welcome to my world. Trying to figure out a gift for a person who has more than I do takes a lot of wine. I'm too drunk to shop, here's a card."

(159)
"Be brave. You're old now."

(160)
"Do you know why we drink on our birthday, cause it's the only way to face the truth. We suck. We're old. Happy truth day."

(161)
"Start your special day with a facial, cause wow, those wrinkles."

(162)
"Six degrees of separation makes you related to some gorgeous model somewhere. Enjoy this crap, it ain't true."

(163)
"Don't lie about your age; we can see your face. Happy reality day."

(164)
"Face the truth, you ain't no young buck; you're the old guy hunting the young buck who never catches it. Happy old day."

(165)
"Grumpy cat said you're old, why celebrate that. He also said, don't come over unless you like being ignored."

(166)
"Your life is just starting out, you have so much ahead of you. Buckle up, that trip can be hell. Here's to the seat-belts of life."

(167)
"Happy B-day. When you get arrested, call me, I'll tweet about it."

(168)
"You're celebrating your countdown; I don't get that. Happy closer-to-your-exit day."

(169)
"Stay sharp, read books, or something. You're not getting younger; you're slowly rotting from the inside. Too real? Sorry, your insides look like a lovely rose bush. Thorny and shriveling."

(170)
"It's none of my business, but your birthday is filled with holes; did the stork bring you, because whoa, your mother looks younger than you do! On the bright side, you'll look better as you age."

(171)
"The number of candles on your cake requires three fire extinguishers and five really hot firefighters. Thank gawd you're old as dirt."

(172)
"We called the fire department, rehearsed our safety evacuation plan, and I still lost my eyebrows lighting your cake."

(173)
"Long gone is the day your virginal self can brag about purity. You can lie about it. Do that. Don't listen to nasty me. Happy it's-gone-forever day."

(174)
"Save yourself. Don't celebrate."

(175)
"You still have time to reach for the stars. Just put a little arthritis cream on first, then change your pee-pad. After that, reach, then rest for three hours. Happy star-reaching-is-exhausting day."

(176)
"I'm casting a spell on you. Bring me cash so I can buy you a gift. Poof."

(177)
"If you're a witch, I'm a witch. If you're a son-of-witch, that makes you a warlock. I'm not a warlock. You win. Happy spell day."

(178)
"Dream on. It's all that's left."

(179)
"You're ten birthday's away from becoming a crazy-cat-lady. Stay cat-less for as long as you can, cats age you!"

(180)
"Be all you can be. Otherwise, I'll be all I can be, and you couldn't handle that kind of competition. Good luck, happy birthday, and I'll see you at the top."

(181)
"You're life is exhausting. Thud; that's me fainting for you. Take a freaking break!"

(182)
"We're drowning in your dust. Show some sympathy, dude. Toss us a bone."

(183)

"You're beautiful, but what's with those feet? Happy not-so-perfect after-all day."

(184)

"Sarcasm is my friend. Do you have any? Here's to getting to know sarcasm better this year."

(185)

"I can do sarcasm. Can you? No, that's right, you're the serious type. Here, I'll try serious; you're so beautiful, I can smell you from here. Happy birthday!"

(186)

"If you're holy, I'm holy. Just my socks though. Happy spiritual day!"

(187)
"We noticed that when you see an obstacle, you just plow over it. Way to scare the crap out of everyone. Happy birthday to the crusher."

(188)
"Your destiny is with me. I'm a freak, be worried. Happy birthday to a fellow freak."

(189)
"You win. You're older than me. I'm trying to wipe that smile off my face. Have a great year as the older and wiser one."

(190)
"Hide! And I'll go seek. Happy B-Day!"

(191)
"So you're not a Tiger in life. Better to be a teddy bear anyway; nobody hunts a teddy bear. Softies rule. Happy birthday to my stuffed buddy."

(192)
"Commonsense on our birthday isn't necessary. Don't listen to that; you'll get arrested."

(193)
"You're old now, and none of it will work. Finally, we're on equal ground. Happy it's-all-busted day."

(194)
"We love you, we like you, we need you. We know you hate that crap. Tough, suck it up buttercup."

(195)
"Go ahead and dance all night long on your birthday. You have to leave the house so it may not happen, right?"

(196)
"We'll rally around you for your birthday. That's what crazy friends do."

(197)
"I'll take all the blame for the crazy on your birthday, but we all know you're the crazier one."

(198)
"Slap your own face before we go out, saves me having to do it later for the crap you're going to pull. Happy birthday trouble."

(199)
"Happy birthday means never having to say you're sorry. Yeah, that ain't gonna fly. Get dressed, bring your sorry face; we're doing the apology tour."

(200)
"Wrap up the pout face and whining. You're old; I'm old. I'm grumpy; you're grumpy. You're wrinkled; I'm wrinkled. We're like two old peas in a shriveled pod."

(201)
"Fake it until you make it. You're 106, for gawd-sakes, I hope it happens soon. Happy birthday to the best faker on the planet."

(202)
"Your life is chaotic, is that why you're a bit looney? Happy birthday, Nutbar."

(203)
"You can't keep having birthdays like this; we like you at this age!"

(204)
"When you grow up, I want to be there to see it for myself!"

(205)
"You can recuse yourself from this birthday!"

(206)
"If you'd like to challenge this birthday, I know a guy."

(207)
"A card, a text, a Facebook post, a tweet, on Instagram, and by email, how many more times do I have to say it! Have a freaking happy birthday beeyatch."

(208)
"Your birthday is one giant stressful event! You're high maintenance, but we love you for that. Leave it to us; we're going to make sure you're treated like a star!"

(209)
"Dreams can come true, but your dreams are freaking ridiculous, cut us average people some slack! We can't do half the *hit on your list!"

(210)
"When life hands you lemons, squish the buggers, and make a pie. Happy birthday to the best lemon destroyer we know."

(211)
"Ignorance is bliss for the ignorant; you must never experience bliss. Sucks to be that smart, doesn't it?"

(212)
"Today, you celebrate another year on Earth. You haven't left the planet in the past year, have you?"

(213)
"Your cake might explode. Skip the candles."

(214)
"Don't tell anyone how old you are. You'll make me look bad!"

(215)
"If you look this good at this age, you must have been a heart-stopping hottie back then. Happy birthday to the only person I know who doesn't age. I hate you."

(216)
"You get one free crazy day. Enjoy your birthday; don't get arrested."

(217)
"They say you're boring. Flip a car over and prove them wrong. You know I'm kidding right? Birthday greetings!"

Cheerful Sayings for a Card

Chapter Five

(218)
"Happy people are fun to be around, that's why we love you the best! We know you'll have a happy birthday because that's how you roll."

(219)
"My smiling face loves your smiling face. Here's to more happiness on your birthday."

(220)
"Let's go out and have the time of our lives on your big day. We know how to live life, and there's nobody I'd rather be with than you."

(221)
"You're the star in my life. Happy Birthday to the brightest light."

(222)
"You're unstoppable when you decide to go for it; we love that about you, happy birthday."

(223)
"You seem to know the secret of life; to face your day with determination and good cheer. Happy birthday."

(224)
"We can't be in a good mood all the time, yet you seem to be. For your birthday, we're going to be more like you."

(225)
"Three cheers for the best person we know, happy birthday."

(226)
"Our home fills up with good energy when you come over; please spend the day with us for your birthday. We want to spoil you to say thanks."

(227)
"Peaceful days and nights are calming. For your birthday, our wish is that you have 365 days like this."

(228)
"You're the reason I survive the tough days in this life. Your optimism and support carry me when I can't go on. Thanks for being the amazing soul you are. Happy birthday to my earth angel."

(229)
"You're the example of what a true friend is. We all want to be more like you. Happy birthday to a person who inspires so many."

(230)
"When I get to the Pearly Gates, and they ask me who was the brightest example of grace in your life, you'll get top billing. Happy birthday to a soul for all souls."

(231)
"Happy birthday to the person who takes away all my doubts and makes me feel whole. Your beautiful nature spreads happiness. Thank you for being there for me."

(232)
"You're not sitting at home for your birthday. I'm dragging your butt out, and we're going to dance till your next birthday! Let's have fun!"

(233)
"You're birthday is like a full bowl of color mixed with a collection of happy faces combined with all the stars in the universe. I know, corny to the max, but I mean it; we love celebrating you and your wonderful life."

(234)
"Jump up and down, we are! It's your birthday and the perfect reason to wear our work-out bras."

(235)
"Put on your safety gear, this birthday party is going to shake the house, and mess your hair."

(236)
"Alright, let's get this celebration going! Your birthday gives us another reason to be happy, like we needed another."

(237)
"Don't blink, another year just flew by, and you're still the classiest one of all. Happy birthday to the one we all look up to."

(238)
"We're crashing your life, we want to be you!"

(239)
"Smile, smile, smile, that's the rule on your birthday. You're used to that anyway. That's what we love about you; you're upbeat nature."

(240)
"We're sending you good cheer, good vibes and good thoughts on your birthday. You deserve all that and more for being the first-class person you are."

(241)
"This card is the lamest thing to give to someone who fills our life with joy and purpose. We would give you the moon if we could. Happy birthday to the most beautiful person we know."

(242)
"If you're not careful we'll come over there and show you what a real party looks like!"

(243)
"Dreams come true when we believe in ourselves. We're hoping you have a year of solid believe in yourself because you're pretty damned amazing. Nobody deserves success more than you do, happy birthday."

(244)
"I coming over to give you the biggest birthday hug on the planet. Get ready for smiles, hugs, wine, and cake. Oh, and I'm bringing ten of your closest friends."

(245)

"Happy birthday to the person who brings joy to the world. We think they wrote that song for you. It fits."

(246)

"You don't seem to know how special you are. Happy birthday to the Queen of earth."

(247)

"You're another year older, yet seem like you're another year younger. Makes me so jealous! If you get any younger, I'll have to change your diaper. Happy birthday to the person who inspires us all to stay healthy and young at heart."

(248)
"Your heart is bigger than most, and we're grateful for all you do and for who you are. Thanks for bringing cheer into the lives of everyone you meet."

(249)
"You are on your way to greatness, just one question, can you take us with you?"

(250)
"Eating cake on your birthday seems so trivial compared to the amazing person you are. Maybe you should eat 100 cakes. That's the reward you deserve for being awesome."

(251)
"You are my truth. You are my soul. You are my hope. I don't mean to put pressure on you, just wanted to let you know how much you mean to me."

(252)
"I've been thinking about how my soul has held up this long without you by my side every day. Maybe we were meant to be apart like this so I could learn to be stronger. Whatever the reason the universe decided we should be apart, on your birthday, I'm sending love and thanks to that universe for bringing you into my life. You've made me who I am, and you've helped me to have courage. My heart needed to find courage. I love you, happy birthday."

(253)
"On your birthday, the world needs to stop for a minute and bow down to your goodness. You deserve that much."

(254)
"Have you ever considered giving life lessons to the rest of us on this planet? You've mastered all the tough stuff, and we could use your tips. Happy birthday to the wise one."

(255)
"Look in the mirror and tell me what you see; is it a happy, honest, kind, amazing, generous, successful, wise, and smart person? If not, it's someone else's reflection, because that's who you are to us."

(256)

"Your guardian angel said she's bored. Apparently, you're such a goodie-two-shoes she has nothing to do! I told her to get her wings on, I'm taking you out for your birthday, and she's gonna need to do some fast flying to keep up."

(257)

"You're the only person I know who can take a wonderful day like your birthday and turn it into a problem. Oops, that's a similar thing Linus said to Charlie Brown. Let's go out and change your stars. Oops, that's a similar thing that was said in the movie a Knight's Tale. Well, you get it, let's do this!"

(258)
"Your birthday is a chance for me to tell you what I've wanted to tell you for years; you're more than just a friend, you hold a piece of me and will own that piece for this lifetime and all the ones to come."

(259)
"I think we met in 1612, then again in 1789, then again in 1895, and we're together again in this lifetime. Can't you do anything without me? Actually, I can't do this human life stuff without you. Thanks for being by my side for the past 400 years or so. I wonder what our next great adventure will be in the next 100 years or so? I think we'll be space explorers. I'll drive. Happy birthday to my fellow time traveler."

(260)

"Your life story is like something out of a romantic novel. You've got the job, the love of your life, an amazing family, and a best friend who adores you. I do love being that friend. Happy birthday to the one who has it all."

(261)

"We wanted to write happy birthday to you in the sky, but the entire sky is booked. The world needs to know all about your awesomeness!"

(262)

"A little birdie, doggie, rabbit, and kitty informed us that it was your birthday today. They remembered we didn't. No wonder I'm not a pet. Have a great year coming up!"

(263)

"Pains me to say it, but your life is an example for all of us. You've tackled things head on and deserve only good things. Happy birthday to the best life teacher."

(264)

"Being yourself has proven to be a successful approach to life. Congratulations on embracing who you are. We love your approach and your energy! Happy birthday."

(265)

"It's a brave new world, and we're sending you love and good wishes for the year ahead. We know you'll tackle anything you face. Happy birthday."

(266)
"We love how you approach life, with a smile and with grace. We could all take a lesson from you. Happy birthday."

(267)
"We took a vote and decided you should be our leader. Let us know when you want to have a meeting. We'll take orders and do what you say for just one day on your birthday."

(268)
"When you've reached your limit, come over, and I'll spoil you rotten. I know you'll never come over because your life is almost damned perfect. Congratulations on mastering yourself and have a great year ahead."

About The Author

At the time of writing, I'm a 59-year-old mother of 4 grown sons, a stepmother to three grown kids, and, to-date, a step-grandmother to 5 beautiful children.

My professional background has been in telecommunications, real estate, as well as owning two websites: one relating to home décor called, Funkthishouse.com, and the other to do with the emotion in songs, Drageda.com – The Heart of Country Music. I also have several articles featured on Hubpages. (hubpages.com/@brite-ideas).

I completed my first book in October 2019. It's a book of personal poems spanning fifty years, called *We Will Have Morning Smiles*. I also finished the second book in that same month called *#Stumped, Instant Party Riddles for Teens and Adults*. I recently completed a third book called *What to Write in a Love Card*.

Why A Book About Sayings for Cards?

I've been writing sayings for cards for decades. Most of those sayings can be found in personally authored online articles or on various pages on my website Drageda.com.

The ability to toss out one-liners appears to be genetic. One of my brothers possesses the crazy skill of blurting out one-liners at will. It seems I've inherited the written version of this genetic anomaly. Just hand me a keyboard, give me a topic, and the sayings find their way to the page.

That's where the idea for *Sayings for Cards* was born. I thought, what the heck, let's get all these things out of my head and into a book, eBook, or website. I hope you find a saying or two for your birthday card or text.

Thank You for Reading

Thanks kindly for taking the time to read or scroll through *"What to Write in a Birthday Card."* Time is our most precious commodity, and I appreciate your giving a bit of yours to this book. If today is your birthday, happy birthday :)

Manufactured by Amazon.ca
Bolton, ON